All God Created You to Be:

Journey to Identity

Christine Casten and Shelley White

Radiant Brilliance, LLC
ISBN-13 978-0692276051 (Radiant Brilliance, LLC)
ISBN-10 069227605x

Copyright © 2014 Christine Casten and Shelley White

All rights reserved. No part of this book may be reproduced, stored in a retrieval system or transmitted in any form or by any means whether scanned, electronic, mechanical, photocopy, recording, or otherwise, without prior written permission of the copyright owner, except by the reviewer who wishes to quote a brief passage in connection with a review for inclusion in a magazine, newspaper or broadcast. The use of short quotations or occasional page copying for personal or group study is permitted. This book may not be reprinted for commercial gain or profit.

All scripture is taken from the New King James Version®. Copyright © 1982 by Thomas Nelson, Inc. Used by permission. All rights reserved.

Cover and book design: Teresa Lickliter, Frisco, Texas

Requests for information should be emailed to:
allgodcreated@gmail.com or visit the website at www.allgodcreatedbook.com

Endorsements

"One of the enemy's greatest attacks against us as believers is in the area of our identity. Every man and woman has struggled with such things as insecurity, low self esteem, value, at one time or another. Regardless of how long you have been a Christian, this study will bring greater insight and revelation and help you establish who you are in Christ. The format makes it perfect for personal study as well as small groups or mentoring ministries."

Adana Wilson
Associate Pastor of Adult Ministries,
Gateway Church

"In this study guide the reader is taken on a personal journey of discovery and intimacy with God. The reader is challenged to think creatively and understand their true position in Christ. I highly recommend All God Created You to Be: Journey to Identity *as a superb guide for study groups and workshops."*

Pastor Brenda P. Lockley
Co-Pastor DeKalb Christ Assembly
Founder/President Living Bread Ministries

All God Created You to Be: Journey to Identity *is a devotional study that helps a person encounter God and His truth in ways that can lead to transformational change. Christine and Shelley share insights on every page of the book, and their questions help a person to personally encounter the Holy Spirit through His Word. If you are looking for a clear path to understand who you are in Christ, then* All God Created You to Be: Journey to Identity *is the Bible study for you."*

Marc Fey
Marketing and non-profit executive,
Leadership coach, and
author of The 2:10 Project

"For the person seeking to dig deeper into their place in God's heart and in this world, I highly recommend All God Created You to Be: Journey to Identity *as a great resource for study and contemplation."*

Sheri Sims
Founder Godhearted Ministries

"I recommend All God Created You to Be: Journey to Identity *as it will take you on a journey to finding your true identity which will lead to more intimacy and more healing in your walk with God."*

Barbara Rodriguez
Founder, Refuge City and RC Outreach

Dedication

This study is dedicated to my precious Lord. Because of Him, I learn to see the world, others and myself from His perspective. I am thankful this journey is never ending, amazing and always an adventure! I am blessed by my family and friends who share my story and journey. To my husband, John, who is my perfect match and can always make me laugh. To my incredible kids who help me see life in new ways! To my family and friends, who have offered prayer, encouragement, feedback, hope, stretching, laughter and unconditional support in my life.   To all of you, I am so grateful that you are in my life! This study guide is also dedicated to the ones who will go through it. May you deepen in the Lord and become *All God Created You to Be.*

Christine Casten

My gratitude and love go to the following:

To my Lord and Savior Jesus Christ who held my hand and taught me the things written in this study. A journey of finding my true self; a journey I will continue on until He takes me home. To all our children; may you continually grow in the knowledge and understanding of the Lord. May you always have an insatiable hunger for the Lord and never stop seeking Him. He will show you great and marvelous things. Jordan and Madison you are my greatest earthly joy! My husband who always sees me as Christ sees me; encouraging me and supporting me as I step out in faith to my calling. My friends who have prayed, cried, laughed and encouraged me along this journey of life. I treasure you all. Finally to the reader of this study; may you be richly blessed with a greater understanding of who you are through Christ and step out in boldness in your new found identity as you become all God created you to be!

Shelley White

All God Created You to Be: Journey to Identity

Contents

Part 1- Foundations

Starting Out: My View - 12

Who Is God
    Goodness of God - 16
    Provider - 20
    Protector and Deliverer - 24
    Healer - 28
    Promise Keeper - 32

Knowing God
    Vastness of God - 36
    Dialogue with God - 40
    Friend of God - 44
    How Knowing God Helps Me Know Me - 48

Part 2- Discovering Your Unique Identity

Inheritance of Believers
    Infinite Yet Personal - 54
    Shared Identity 1 - 58
    Shared Identity 2 - 62

Personal Inheritance
    From Friend of God to Bride of Christ - 66
    Personal Identity - 70
    Learning Who You Are/Inheritance -74
    Confidence in Identity -78

Challenges and Identity
    Dealing with Internal Negatives - 82
    Adversity and Identity - 86

Faith Walk
    Faith Strengtheners/Altar Stone Memorials - 90
    Destiny Calling -94

Making the Most of *All God Created You to Be: Journey to Identity*

All God Created You to Be: Journey to Identity encourages you to deepen your relationship with God and discover your exceptional design. Through this study you will discover how God offers countless ways to embrace more of who He is and understand how He created YOU!

Part 1: Foundations starts with a snapshot of where you are in your walk with God and inspires new understanding about God's nature; building your faith and strengthening the way you see God in your life. The focus then shifts to your relationship and personal communication with the Lord from the perspective of your identity in Christ.

Part 2: Discovering Your Unique Identity launches your personal discovery process. Recognizing who you are in Jesus creates a sense of purpose and builds trust in Him, as well as confidence in your God given identity. This section highlights the difference between a shared and individual identity, identity confidence, how to respond to external adversity and internal obstacles, and how to actively step into your calling.

All God Created You to Be is designed for a variety of needs including study groups, mentor/coach relationships and/or as a personal devotional.

What to expect: Each weekly topic is divided into the sections below

Stand on it! *highlights the Bible verse on which the topic is based.*

Think on it! *expands and develops the topic by breaking it down, offering points for consideration and providing real life examples.*

Unpack it! *provides a place for discussion and an opportunity to share your thoughts on the topic, points of consideration, or "aha" moments you may be experiencing.*

Embrace it! *places major points of the topic at the feet of Jesus and offers a place of thankfulness to God and encouragement for you on the journey.*

Explore it! *creates space for your personal growth to continue. The Bible verses and questions offer an opportunity for you to spend time with the Lord exploring the topic in more depth, journaling your thoughts and recording anything the Lord reveals in that process. Groups and mentor/coaching relationships may choose to use these questions as additional discussion questions at the next meeting.*

Act on it! *offers a moment to think about a treasure God highlighted for you through this lesson and how you will apply it to your daily life. Just for a moment, think about how you can integrate this treasure in your life and live it out. This section can be used as an accountability piece for groups to discuss how the process of living out this treasure is going.*

Part 1:
Foundations

Starting Out: My View

Stand on it! *"So he answered and said, "'You shall love the Lord your God with all your heart, with all your soul, with all your strength, and with all your mind,' and, 'your neighbor as yourself.'"* Luke 10:27

Think on it! Take a picture of yourself at this moment in time! SNAP! What do you see? Where you are in this moment is a point on your journey. It is a moment where your past merges into your future.

Our experiences affect how we relate to God. For many, it takes time to realize past experiences and self-views color our understanding of the Father's love. Focusing on regrets for past decisions turn our eyes away from what God is saying and speaking over us. Shame and hurt hold us captive in those past decisions and life circumstances. Holding on to past hurts, disappointments and struggles, blinds us from seeing God in His true nature and character. Removing the blinders allows us to move forward into the process of discovering the goodness of God and realizing how excellent God is at shifting our viewpoint; even turning past negatives into areas of personal strength.

The way you view God affects how you see life. If you see Him as a distant God, uninvolved in the details of life, the idea of interacting with Him is a foreign concept. If you see Him as your caring Father who is interactive and present, you will see Him active in the minute parts of your life and in all things around you. The lifestyle that comes out of loving God with every part of yourself brings a renewed understanding of His devotion to your growth and your communication with Him.

Unpack it!

How do you see yourself? What are your best qualities? What are your biggest challenges?

_____
_____
_____
_____
_____
_____

What do you think a perfect father would do or act like?

_____
_____
_____

What is your perception of God? How could seeing God as a perfect father shift or change your current view of Him?

_____
_____
_____
_____

Where is your relationship with God? How would you describe Him? How do you see Him? Close, distant, angry, loving?

_____
_____
_____
_____
_____
_____
_____
_____
_____
_____
_____
_____
_____
_____
_____

Embrace it!

Thank You Lord, for dying on the cross for me so I can have everlasting life, and that my past no longer defines who I am. It is the past and we know all things work for the good for those who love You. I am a new creation in Christ. Father, You are the perfect parent and know every tear I shed and every hair on my head. You give Your angels charge over me and that gives me great comfort Lord. Thank You for the life You have for me: plans to prosper not harm me, plans to give me a hope and a future. Father, I know You will never leave me or forsake me and I will always be Your beloved. I love You, Lord.

Explore it! Read these scriptures and explore what you see God revealing to you through the verses. Take some time to write down your thoughts.

Read 2 Corinthians 3:16-18. By removing the veil(s), or blinders in your life, Jesus takes you through a transformation process of becoming more like Him. His Spirit brings freedom. What do you think His "freedom" means for you? Describe what you think a life of freedom would look like.

_____
_____
_____
_____
_____
_____
_____
_____
_____
_____
_____
_____
_____
_____
_____
_____
_____
_____
_____
_____
_____
_____
_____
_____
_____
_____
_____
_____
_____
_____

Read Luke 12:32. The Father delights in giving you the best of Himself. He desires to wipe away the fear that comes from misperceptions of His character and replace it with a "fear" of respecting Him and knowing more deeply the Goodness He desires to share with you. Ask God to pinpoint misperceptions you hold about Him. List those misperceptions and what you see as His true nature. How have those misperceptions created barriers in your relationship with Him?

_____
_____
_____
_____
_____
_____
_____
_____
_____
_____
_____
_____
_____
_____
_____
_____
_____
_____
_____
_____
_____
_____
_____
_____
_____
_____
_____

Act on it! God placed treasures in this lesson. What treasure is He offering to you today? How do you think you might apply this treasure to your daily life?

Who is God: Goodness of God

Stand on it! *"But the fruit of the spirit is love, joy, peace, longsuffering, kindness, goodness, faithfulness, gentleness, self-control. Against such there is no law." Galatians 5:22-23*

Think on it! God is good. Sometimes things happen in life that make us question this statement. But His word says that He is for us and wants to prosper us. Even when we face challenges and hurtful experiences, He has the ability to help us turn that negative experience into a source of forgiveness and strength.

It is for freedom's sake that Jesus set us free! (Galatians 5:1) His goodness established a plan for reconnection to Him after sin separated us from Him. His goodness is what calls us to Him. His goodness describes who He is, His actions and His nature. The passage above describes His goodness as the fruit of the Spirit. These are the attributes used to describe Him time and again throughout all scripture.

Unpack it!

Do you perceive God's goodness in all things, good or bad? Explain.

_____
_____
_____
_____
_____
_____
_____
_____
_____

Have you struggled to believe God's goodness is at work in all parts of your own life? Why?

_____
_____
_____
_____
_____
_____
_____
_____
_____

Think of a difficulty you have faced where it was hard to see God's goodness in the midst of crisis. Looking back to that time, can you pinpoint areas where God's goodness was at work? What are they?

_____
_____
_____
_____
_____
_____
_____
_____
_____
_____
_____
_____
_____
_____
_____
_____
_____
_____
_____

How do you tie the fruit of the Spirit (in Galatians 5:16-26) together with the goodness of God?

_____
_____
_____
_____
_____

Embrace it!
Thank You Father, for loving me so much that You sent Your only Son to die for my sins so I can have everlasting life with You! Thank You for freedom from bondage through the blood of Jesus that I may have Your fruit of the Spirit; embracing Your 'love, joy, peace, kindness, goodness, faithfulness, gentleness and self control.' Thank You for choosing me, never leaving me or forsaking me! Your mercies are new every morning. Great is Your faithfulness! Thank You, Lord.

Explore it!

Read Exodus 33. Moses asked to see God's glory. God responds that He will allow His goodness to pass before Moses. But because Moses was unable to handle the fullness of God, God revealed only what Moses could receive. God knows our capacity and protects us from the full onslaught that comes in each situation. How did the goodness of God allow Moses to be protected as God's glory passed? How has the goodness of God allowed you to be protected in your life?

Read Exodus 33 again. Focus on verse 17. God is your perfect Father who knows you personally, by name. He is pleased with you and He knows you as you are. Your thoughts, actions, decisions and even your quirks do not surprise Him. He delights in who you are and how you are made. His desire is for your growth and He longs to see you embrace who you are becoming in Him. Does knowing God accepts the deepest part of who you are allow you to feel greater acceptance? What thoughts and emotions do you experience through this revelation?

_____

Act on it! God placed treasures in this lesson. What treasure is He offering to you today? How do you think you might apply this treasure to your daily life?

Who is God: Provider

Stand on it! *"Every good gift and every perfect gift is from above, and comes down from the Father of lights, with whom there is no variation or shadow of turning."*
James 1:17

Think on it! God still moves mountains. He always provides a way out of any situation. Sometimes He steps in and supernaturally removes the issue. Other times He grants strategy to our hearts on how to overcome the difficult situation or circumstance. Testimonies from today include provision for finances, job opportunities, better health or healing, and safety in dangerous situations. Sometimes money shows up in the mailbox. Other times, He provides a contact or divine appointment for you to step into a better situation. Being vigilant in prayer and in listening for His direction helps us recognize His provision.

The most significant provision He offers is reconciliation to Him. Reconciliation, in this case, is about restoring the relationship between God and man. Sometimes this provision is called being "saved" or "salvation." The basic idea is that Jesus offers the opportunity for man to communicate directly with God again. When we have been reconciled, we can tap into His direction and leading to recognize the provision He offers. Through salvation, we acknowledge and submit to His sovereignty. Through salvation, we have an open invitation to communicate with God in a way a son or daughter communicates with his/her parents. Our best strategy includes willingness to know His ways and learn His heart so that we can follow His leading.

Unpack it!

Share times you have struggled with having faith that the Lord would provide?

_____
_____
_____
_____
_____
_____
_____
_____
_____
_____
_____

During those times, did you recognize encouragement the Lord released (through scripture, prayer, someone's encouragement, etc.)? What was it?

_____
_____
_____
_____
_____
_____
_____
_____

Why was the most significant provision He gives reconciliation? What does reconciliation mean to you?

_____
_____
_____
_____
_____
_____
_____
_____

Why does knowing His ways and His heart create a good life strategy?

_____
_____
_____
_____
_____
_____
_____
_____

Embrace it!
Thank you, Father, for being the perfect provider. You provided Your Son even when I did not realize I had a need; allowing me access to Your blessings that come down from the heavenly lights. I am grateful You hear my prayers and guide me daily along the journey. Praise You! You are a Father that never changes; who provides for all of my needs according to Your riches in Christ Jesus. I love you Lord.

Explore it!

Read Philippians 4:19. God meets ALL our needs: emotional, physical, spiritual, financial and relational. What do you think "the riches of His glory" means? How does God meet your needs?

Read Luke 11:28. What is the significance of both hearing and obeying? Does hearing from God require a response? What role does reconciliation (salvation) play in hearing from God?

_____

Act on it! God placed treasures in this lesson. What treasure is He offering to you today? How do you think you might apply this treasure to your daily life?

Who is God: Protector and Deliverer

Stand on it! *"Because he has set his love upon Me, therefore I will deliver him; I will set him on high, because he has known My name."* Psalms 91:14

Think on it! God promises to protect and deliver His children. The timing of His deliverance can vary. It can come before, during, or even after a situation. He also delivers us from ourselves and our negative mindsets or destructive habits. We do not always know when the deliverance will occur, but He WILL step in and help us through the process of growth. That point often begins when we acknowledge His name and surrender to Him.

We all face times when we want God's protection. At times it seems like He is not protecting us. Looking back, however, we may realize how His protection was active in some way the whole time. Other times, it is very obvious through the situation that God's hand covers us. We rest inside His place of refuge.

Learning to trust His wisdom in our protection is one of the biggest challenges we face. Past situations of hurt may make us wonder why He did not step in at that moment. The "why" questions are usually not answered in our lives here on earth. However, He often will answer these questions: "What do I need to do with this?" "How should I go forward?" "What are you trying to teach me in this situation?" And "How can I help others who have had similar experiences?"

Unpack it!

Share one or two experiences when you have seen God's protection in your life.

_____
_____
_____
_____
_____
_____
_____
_____
_____
_____

How is "acknowledging His name" a significant part of the "Stand On It" verse for this lesson?

_____
_____
_____
_____
_____
_____
_____

Why do you think God sometimes intervenes prior to a situation and waits to intervene in others?

_____
_____
_____
_____
_____
_____
_____

Have you ever had an experience where you know God delivered you? What happened?

_____
_____
_____
_____
_____
_____
_____
_____
_____
_____
_____
_____
_____

Embrace it!
My Lord, thank You for Your loving protection. Under Your wings, I shall take refuge. You give Your angels charge over me, and come to my rescue time and time again! I shall not be afraid. You are my shield and buckler. Your deliverance has set me free from my old ways. You are my Lord and salvation.

Explore it!

Read Psalms 91:11-12. Have you ever considered the many times God intervened to protect you before you realized the danger? Recognizing God's protection from unknown dangers is an active part of your life. How does this affect your understanding of His love for you? Does this revelation change your perception of God's protection and deliverance in your life?

___
___
___
___
___
___
___
___
___
___
___
___
___
___
___
___
___
___
___
___
___
___
___
___
___
___
___
___
___
___
___
___
___

Read John 14:16-17. What role do you think the Holy Spirit offers in your deliverance and protection? What is your role in being protected by the Lord? Why is it important to develop your ability to recognize the Holy Spirit's voice or prompting in your daily life?

_____
_____
_____
_____
_____
_____
_____
_____
_____
_____
_____
_____
_____
_____
_____
_____
_____
_____
_____
_____

Act on it! God placed treasures in this lesson. What treasure is He offering to you today? How do you think you might apply this treasure to your daily life?

Who is God: Healer

Stand on it! *"He heals the brokenhearted and binds up their wounds."* Psalms 147:3

Think on it! God is able to heal us. We often focus on God healing a physical need. Testimonies, or personal experiences, do exist of His healing power mending physical wounds. However, He also repairs our broken hearts and emotions: bringing restoration to the point where we are operating in full health.

The process of emotional healing may take time. Our culture tells us to "buck it up" or "stuff them (emotions) down" pretending they are not a problem anymore. However, negative emotions and memories do affect our lives, causing us to react to situations with extreme sensitivity or a skewed sense of reality. Many of our negative life habits stem from hurts and wounds of the past.

God's plan is for our best. (Jeremiah 29:11) He desires for us to walk in fullness and wholeness. The death and resurrection of Jesus granted Him the authority to "exchange" our burden for His. (Matthew 11:30) He takes our sin, emotional hurts and physical needs on Himself while *exchanging* them for His healing and emotional strength. As we spend time with Him, sometimes areas of hurt or wounding may come to mind. Each time something comes to mind, we have the opportunity to offer those things to Him and ask Him to make an "exchange" with us.

Unpack it! Below is a prayer tool for making this "exchange" with the Lord. (Sensitivity alert: Due to the nature of this exercise, group leaders may want the group to break into pairs or allow members to go through it outside of the group setting.)

Do any specific emotional wounds come to mind as you read the "Think On It!" section? If you feel comfortable, share one of them.

_____
_____
_____
_____
_____
_____
_____
_____

Pray with a partner and ask the Lord to reveal His heart in that situation.

___

If you are ready to release that burden to Him: Invite Him to remove the hurt.
Then ask Him what He will replace that burden with in your heart.

___

Wait on the Lord to understand what He returned to you in this "exchange."
Share what the Lord revealed to you. (repeat this process for any other wounds the Lord brings to your heart.)

___

Embrace it!
Lord Jesus, thank You for taking all my pain, suffering, sickness, and sin when You died on the cross for me. Lord, search my heart and, if there is anything that is unpleasing to You, please reveal it so I can be free from that burden. Jesus, I now lay all my sorrows and sickness at the foot of the cross and in exchange I receive Your love and Your healing. You, not the world, are the balm to my wounds. Thank You for giving me a new heart and mind in Christ.

Explore it!

In the verse: *"Beloved, I pray that you may prosper in all things and be in health, just as your soul prospers."* (3 John 1:2), John links the prosperity of our lives with the health of our "soul." Spend some time with the Lord exploring what this means in your life.

_____
_____
_____
_____
_____
_____
_____
_____
_____
_____
_____
_____
_____
_____
_____
_____
_____
_____
_____
_____
_____
_____
_____
_____
_____
_____
_____
_____
_____
_____
_____
_____

John 10:10 states: *"The thief does not come except to steal, and to kill, and to destroy. I have come that they may have life, and that they may have it more abundantly."* Physical ailments, emotional strain and spiritual pain are not part of the fullness God desires for you. Explore what you understand living a life of fullness in Christ means. Ask God to expand your understanding and journal what He releases to your heart.

_____
_____
_____
_____
_____
_____
_____
_____
_____
_____
_____
_____
_____
_____
_____
_____
_____
_____
_____
_____
_____
_____
_____
_____
_____
_____
_____
_____
_____

Act on it! God placed treasures in this lesson. What treasure is He offering to you today? How do you think you might apply this treasure to your daily life?

Who is God: Promise Keeper

Stand on it! *"Let us hold fast the confession of our hope without wavering, for He who promised is faithful."* Hebrews 10:23

Think on it! God is a promise keeper. *"For all the promises of God in Him are Yes, and in Him Amen, to the glory of God through us."* (2 Corinthians 1:20) The testimony of God (in the Bible) is the story of how God's promises have held true. His words are not void and do not fall to the ground. (Isaiah 55:11) In other words, His words have meaning and will remain.

When He makes a promise, He keeps it. Nothing on earth or in heaven can change it or negate the contract He makes when He speaks. He knows the end from the beginning and works to make all His promises come to pass. He has many promises over the people of the earth, the earth itself and the spiritual realm. He also has promises He has spoken over you.

Part of our walk with God is a chance to understand those promises in our lives. As we learn to recognize the promises He has for us, we learn to identify when those promises are completed. By identifying the promises and then seeing them happen, our faith is built and our story, or testimony, can encourage others around us.

Unpack it!

How do you feel knowing God keeps the promises He made in the Bible?

_____
_____
_____
_____
_____
_____

What Biblical promises give you the most peace and comfort?

_____
_____
_____
_____
_____
_____

Knowing His word does not come back "void", have you ever spoken His word out loud to remind you of His promises? What specific scriptures/promises do you pray? If you have never practiced speaking scripture out loud, find a verse and practice speaking it back to God.

_____
_____
_____
_____
_____
_____
_____
_____
_____
_____

What promises has God spoken over you or in you? What scriptures support those promises? Locate/recite these verses and speak them out loud. If you do not know, take your favorite verse and think/share about the promise God has in it for you.

_____
_____
_____
_____
_____
_____
_____
_____
_____
_____
_____
_____

Embrace it!
Father, thank You for being a God who is the same: yesterday, today and forever. You are a Father that does not lie and stands by what He says. Lord, help me believe in Your word and let it be written in my heart. I seek comfort under the shadow of Your wings, Lord, knowing what Your word says is true for me. I will stand firm on Your promises today and forever more.

Explore it!

"In the hope of eternal life, which God, who cannot lie, promised before time began." (Titus 1:2) God's promises are eternal. He does not lie nor does He forget His words. Since He does not forget, why is it important to speak God's word back to Him? What benefit does speaking His promises out loud bring a believer?

_____

Read Isaiah 55. Underline all the scriptures that highlight God's promises. Write out those promises and speak them in your prayer time over the next week.

_____

Act on it! God placed treasures in this lesson. What treasure is He offering to you today? How do you think you might apply this treasure to your daily life?

Knowing God: The Vastness of God

Stand on it! *"How precious also are Your thoughts to me, O God! How great is the sum of them! If I should count them, they would be more in number than the sand; When I awake, I am still with You."* Psalms 139:17-18

Think on it! We struggle to wrap our minds around who God is. He is beyond our understanding or capacity to know, and yet, He desires to reveal Himself to us. The joy of our journey is embracing the revelation He continuously brings of who He is throughout our life. The highest calling we have on our life is to interact with Him while pouring into a dynamic relationship with Him.

The three aspects of God as Father, Son and Spirit offer revelation on community, interaction, unity and purpose. His nature is revealed through the interaction we have with each aspect of God. The "names" of God provide insight into His personality through unconditional love, forgiveness, healing and protection.

God knows He is overwhelming, so He reveals small pieces of Himself through the different seasons of our lives. He teaches us by expanding what we know and adding to our experience of Him. The more we learn, the more our faith is built and the greater level of confidence we have in Him and His ways.

Unpack it!

Do you struggle to understand the Trinity: One God in three aspects of Father, Son and Holy Spirit? Explain how you understand the Trinity.

_____
_____
_____
_____
_____
_____
_____

How can you encourage your dynamic relationship with God?

_____
_____
_____
_____
_____

What aspects of Himself has God revealed to you in the recent past?

What aspects of Himself is God revealing to you today?

Embrace it!
Thank you for being a God that is so big I cannot even fathom everything about You. Your love is mighty and saves. You rejoice over me with gladness! You are merciful, gracious, slow to anger and abounding in steadfast love and faithfulness. Your thoughts and ways are not mine; yet You reveal more of Yourself each day. I hunger to know all of You, my mighty Savior.

Explore it!

Read Isaiah 40:8-14. Focus on the everlasting promise and expansive nature of God. What does the description bring to mind? How does it make you feel about God's majesty? Focus on the shepherd imagery. What does knowing the Lord as your shepherd mean to you? How does the interaction of the shepherd with the sheep reflect His interaction with you?

Read Psalms 139:1-18. This passage highlights God's continued presence in your life. No matter what the situation has been, good or bad, He is near at hand to comfort and speak to you. He formed you and created you. As you read this passage, what do you think about God's desire to be with you? Because He is with you continually, how can you communicate with Him and interact with His presence in a more consistent way?

_____
_____
_____
_____
_____
_____
_____
_____
_____
_____
_____
_____
_____
_____
_____
_____
_____
_____
_____
_____
_____
_____
_____
_____
_____
_____
_____
_____
_____
_____

Act on it! God placed treasures in this lesson. What treasure is He offering to you today? How do you think you might apply this treasure to your daily life?

Knowing God: Dialogue with God

Stand on it! *"To him the doorkeeper opens, and the sheep hear his voice; and he calls his own sheep by name and leads them out."* John 10:3

Think on it! Have you ever thought about prayer as a conversation with God? Many times we think of prayer as a one-way monologue where we tell God how awful we are and ask Him to fix everything. But, prayer is really supposed to be a two-way conversation with Him. Abraham, Moses, David, Paul, and John (to name a few) record some of their conversations with God throughout the Bible.

One way to think about communicating with God is to think of a growing and dynamic relationship between a person and "the ultimate" mentor. He speaks wisdom, strategy, love, encouragement, etc. into our hearts and helps us grow at the speed we are willing to embrace. He opens our thoughts and expands our paradigms of thinking to know Him better. As we learn more of Him and His ways, we also learn more about ourselves and how He created us.

One challenge people share in hearing God is the difficulty that comes from recognizing His "voice." Often, our own expectations of *how* God speaks, creates a barrier. We think the voice of God is a type of "burning bush" experience, a loud booming announcer, or something we have seen in movies. However, the majority of times, it is more like Elijah's experience in the cave (1 Kings 19) when God's voice was a still, small voice. Typically, it is something released in our hearts rather than outside of us. As we continue to practice hearing Him, we learn to discern His "voice" from our own and from the voice of the enemy. His voice never speaks contrary to His word (the Bible). It loves, encourages, offers hope and is personal. Your voice tends to want attention, self-glory, is analytical, and self-promoting. The enemy's voice lies, devalues, condemns, confuses and is demanding. As you practice hearing responses to your prayers, weigh them with these descriptions to determine the source.

Unpack it!

Do you struggle to hear God's voice?

_____
_____
_____
_____
_____

Have you had experiences when you have heard His voice or direction clearly?

___

Do you recognize any obstacles in your life that might keep you from hearing His voice?

___

How do you think removing obstacles will help you hear God's voice better?

___

Embrace it!
Lord, I wake up in the morning and call You by name. Jesus, You answer me. I spend my day listening for Your voice. I focus on what is true and lovely and feel Your love and peace. Thank You, Lord, for being a God who listens and responds to His children, finding it a great pleasure. I knock on Your door and You not only answer, You invite me in to dine at Your table. I long to hear more from You, God.

Explore it!

John 16:12-15 states, *"I still have many things to say to you, but you cannot bear them now. However, when He, the Spirit of truth, has come, He will guide you into all truth; for He will not speak on His own authority, but whatever He hears He will speak; and He will tell you things to come. He will glorify Me, for He will take of what is Mine and declare it to you. All things that the Father has are Mine. Therefore I said that He will take of Mine and declare it to you."* What does this say about ongoing conversations with God? How does the Holy Spirit continue to teach you about the different aspects of God as Jesus and the Father? In what ways do you see that the Holy Spirit has glorified God in your daily life? What truths does He continue to reveal about Jesus and God, the Father in your life?

Read Philippians 4:4-9 and Revelation 3:20. What is your role in prayer? What are the various instructions in Philippians for a believer? What does Philippians encourage you to do with God's truth? What does the Revelations passage promise about relationship with God?

_____

Act on it! God placed treasures in this lesson. What treasure is He offering to you today? How do you think you might apply this treasure to your daily life?

Knowing God: Friend of God

Stand on it! *"Greater love has no one than this, than to lay down one's life for his friend's. You are My friends if you do whatever I command you. No longer do I call you servants, for a servant does not know what his master is doing; but if I have called you friends, for all things that I heard from My Father I have made known to you."*
John 15:13-15

Think on it! God is approachable. When Jesus paid the price for our sins on Calvary, He opened the door to the throne of grace (Hebrews 4:16). We approach it with respect (fear of the Lord) but without shame, reproach, or insecurity. He redeemed us to give us an opportunity to interact with Him. He knows that the wisdom we gain in dialogue with Him keeps us from poor decisions or bad life choices (folly). He wants us to connect with Him, talk with Him and learn from Him. He wants to teach us His ways. His nature is not to teach us in a dictatorial way, but in more of an interactive, exploring way. In other words, He asks us questions and then takes us through the process of exploration to uncover His truths.

The process of conversation with Him opens doors to know Him better, while at the same time, launches us into discovery of who we are in Him and who we were created to be. He likes to answer the questions, "Who are You?" and "Who am I for You?" He is waiting for you to visit with Him and get to know Him better.

Unpack it!

Do you feel like you can approach God with anything? If you were to visualize yourself and God, where is He in relation to you? What type of setting are you in? What do you think is needed for you to take a step closer to Him?

_____
_____
_____
_____
_____
_____
_____
_____
_____
_____

Are you completely transparent when you talk with God? Are there any fears you hold on to that would keep you from having open dialogue with Him? Would you be willing to confess those fears to Him now? If yes, please pray.

_____
_____
_____
_____
_____
_____

Have you had a time when God revealed strategy, wisdom or direction in a specific situation? Did you follow that advice or doubt its source?

_____
_____
_____
_____
_____
_____

Take some time to pray and ask God, "Who are You?" Record His answer below.
(It may come as scripture, words, pictures, music or some other way)

_____
_____
_____
_____
_____
_____
_____
_____
_____
_____
_____

Embrace it!
*Lord, I want to hear Your sweet voice as I go through each day. Open my ears to hear, Lord. Open my eyes to see. Teach me Your ways, Lord. Lead me beside still waters and on paths of righteousness. Hear my cry, God, and attend to my prayer. My heart is overwhelmed at Your unfailing love and mercy.
I will forever be a friend of Yours, Lord.*

Explore it!

Read Judges 6. How did the Angel of the Lord* interact with Gideon at the beginning of the story? What happened after the sacrifice was consumed? How did the Lord continue to communicate with Gideon? *many commentaries describe this angel as the pre-incarnate Christ.

Read 1 Kings 19. Elijah is running scared. He knows Jezebel has killed many of the prophets and thinks he is the only one left. As he goes on this journey, God uses it as an opportunity to teach him about hearing His voice. The Lord provides food for him in verse 6 and then leads him to a place of shelter. Then, He uses a wind, earthquake, fire, and a gentle whisper to teach Elijah. When Elijah heard the gentle word, he got up and went out of the cave.

Why do you think the Lord allowed the wind, earthquake and fire? What do you think caused Elijah to move out of the cave? Why do you think this journey was necessary for Elijah? How do you think his trust in the Lord deepened? Think about your journey. What is God providing, or giving, as you move through your current circumstances. What journey does He have you on so you will be able to recognize His voice? How do you think your trust in the Lord is deepening during this time?

_____
_____
_____
_____
_____
_____
_____
_____
_____
_____
_____
_____
_____
_____
_____
_____
_____
_____
_____
_____
_____
_____
_____
_____

Act on it! God placed treasures in this lesson. What treasure is He offering to you today? How do you think you might apply this treasure to your daily life?

Knowing God: How Knowing God Helps Me Be Me

Stand on it! *"But we all, with unveiled face, beholding as in a mirror the glory of the Lord, are being transformed into the same image from glory to glory, just as by the Spirit of the Lord."* 2 Corinthians 3:18

Think on it! God created you in His own image. That means that He placed characteristics and personality traits in you that reflect who He is. Even though you are uniquely different from anyone else, you were created with certain aspects of His nature. As you learn more about Him and develop a better understanding of His heart, you begin to discover those pieces "of Himself" He put within you.

People emulate what they focus on. For example, when you spend a lot of time with someone, you begin to say phrases they say or pick up mannerisms they have. Just like a couple who has been married for a long time, they often share phrases, mannerisms, and jokes that are specific to the two of them. The more you learn about God's love, the more you begin to adopt His way of seeing both yourself and the world. As you choose to target your mind, will and emotions toward the Lord and spend time in His presence, you will observe more about His heart and ways.

Part One of this study began your Journey to Identity by helping you gain new insight into God's personality, nature and character. As you learned more about Him, you began the process of learning more about yourself. Part 2 continues to build on this journey by giving you tools to discover your Unique Identity and then how to step into your specific calling and purpose. We look forward to continuing the Journey with you!

Unpack it!

What do you think it means to be created in God's image?

_____
_____
_____
_____
_____
_____
_____
_____
_____

What characteristics do you see in you that reflect God's image?

_____
_____
_____
_____
_____
_____
_____
_____
_____
_____.

How does focusing on God allow you to reflect more of who He is through you?

_____
_____
_____
_____
_____

What aspect of God has become more alive or deepened in your understanding through Part 1 of study?

_____
_____
_____
_____
_____
_____
_____
_____
_____
_____

Embrace it!

Father, You created me exceptionally unique, yet in Your image. The more I focus on You and spend time with You, the more I love You. The more I love you, the more I recognize Your desire to release the blessings You have promised me! You are an awesome Father who transforms me into Christ's likeness. Lord, give me Your eyes to see the world and those around me as You do. Let my ways be Your ways and my thoughts your thoughts, Lord! I thank You that I am fearfully and wonderfully made!

Explore it!

Read Philippians 4:8-9, 11-13. This world encourages us to focus on the negatives in our lives. We are constantly bombarded with what we do not have, what we "need" and areas of challenges in our lives. Most choose to focus on the negatives allowing frustration to build and creating a lifestyle of complaint and dissatisfaction. When we focus or "meditate" on the "things that are noble, just, pure, etc." we shift our thoughts to find the perspective of the Lord in all aspects of our lives. As we align our thinking and words with Him, we are able to walk in a greater level of the peace of God. What things did Paul mention that are important to "do"? What is the outcome of a shifted way of thinking? Describe what "living content" in all things looks like or means to you?

_____
_____
_____
_____
_____
_____
_____
_____
_____
_____
_____
_____
_____
_____
_____
_____
_____
_____
_____
_____
_____
_____
_____
_____
_____
_____

Read James 1:2-5. When we allow our way of thinking to align with God's we often see things that were negative as positive. The challenge may not be easy to go through, but knowing and trusting that God will grow you and strengthen you for the journey allows you to see it with a "joyful" mindset. Making the conscious decision to focus on the good of God in a difficult situation can actually create a shift in your internal way of thinking. All of a sudden, it is as if a light shines on that circumstance and you see it from a completely different viewpoint. The frustration, anger, hurt, anxiety, etc. fade away and you are left with peace. Have you ever had this experience? Think of a current situation that seems challenging or hopeless: How can your way of thinking align with God's heart in this situation? How would changing your perspective create hope for that situation? What pure, lovely or noble things can you find in this situation to allow you to count it all joy?

_____
_____
_____
_____
_____
_____
_____
_____
_____
_____
_____
_____
_____
_____
_____
_____
_____
_____
_____
_____
_____
_____
_____
_____
_____
_____
_____

Act on it! God placed treasures in this lesson. What treasure is He offering to you today? How do you think you might apply this treasure to your daily life?

Part 2:

Discovering Your Unique Identity

Inheritance of Believers: Infinite Yet Personal

Stand on it! *"Though the LORD is on high, yet He regards the lowly; but the proud He knows from afar. Though I walk in the midst of trouble, You will revive me; You will stretch out your hand against the wrath of my enemies, and Your right hand will save me. The LORD will perfect that which concerns me; Your mercy, O LORD, endures forever; do not forsake the works of Your hands."* Psalms 138:6-8

Think on it! Thinking of God as infinite and personal presents a paradox. Sometimes it is hard to wrap our minds around the idea of God, infinite creator of the universe, yet also personally involved in the details of our lives. But we find His presence at work in different ways. For example: Sometimes when we pray, we get a "nudging" to look up a certain verse. Or another time we might receive a phone call from a friend at just the right moment with just the right words to encourage us.

Suddenly the God who seems so far away is right there; talking to you directly or through someone else. In the moment we experience His encouragement, we do not always recognize the divine "ordering" of events. He works behind the scenes to bring that moment to pass; His hands at work in your life and the lives of many others.

Unpack it!

What does the paradox of God as infinite, yet, personal mean to you?

_____
_____
_____
_____
_____
_____

Have you ever felt led to look up a scripture, read a specific book or listen to a certain song or album? Did you recognize that this thought or prompting might have been from the Lord? How did God encourage you in that moment?

_____
_____
_____
_____
_____
_____

Share a time when you felt you were alone or that God was not hearing your heart only to see His encouragement show up in an unexpected way.

___

Have you ever thought about the complexity of things God does to meet you in your moment of need? What does this mean to you?

___

Embrace it!
Thank You, Lord, for Your Holy Spirit that dwells in me; Your spirit of truth, my great and mighty comforter, counselor, and redeemer! Out of my heart flows Your living water! You have engraved me in the palms of Your hands; my walls are ever before You. You loved me before time, and I will love You forever more.

Explore it:

Read Romans 8:14. What do you think it means to be "led" or "prompted" by the Spirit of God? Have you ever felt like the Lord was asking you to do or seek out something? Did you act on that feeling?

_____

Read John 6:44-45, Isaiah 54:13. These passages teach that God's children, or those who are Believers of Jesus, will be taught by God. The peace the children experience comes from learning the ways of God and discovering how to live in a deeper level of trust. Do you realize the prompting you feel might be God's attempt to teach you? It might be His encouragement to step into something amazing! What does a personal relationship with God look like to you? What is He teaching you now? How has being taught by God affected the peace in your heart?

_____
_____
_____
_____
_____
_____
_____
_____
_____
_____
_____
_____
_____
_____
_____
_____
_____
_____
_____
_____
_____
_____
_____
_____
_____
_____
_____
_____
_____
_____

Act on it! God placed treasures in this lesson. What treasure is He offering to you today? How do you think you might apply this treasure to your daily life?

Inheritance of Believers: Shared Identity 1

Stand on it! *"Consequently, you are no longer foreigners and strangers, but fellow citizens with God's people and also members of his household, built on the foundation of the apostles and prophets, with Christ Jesus himself as the chief cornerstone. In him the whole building is joined together and rises to become a holy temple in the Lord. And in him, you too are being built together to become a dwelling in which God lives by his spirit."* Ephesians 2:19-22

Think on it! Our Kinship: It is fun to look at family photos. It is amazing how each person is uniquely different, yet shares physical features similar to others in their family. For example, great grandpas, their daughters, and their grandsons may share the same nose and eyes. In addition to physical characteristics, families also share similar personality traits. Those traits seem to appear in most of the family members and continue through the generations. As new family members are born, each one automatically inherits the traits carried in the DNA of prior generations.

As believers, we share similar traits that come from our heavenly Father. Through Christ, our heavenly inheritance binds us to Him and to one another. By accepting Jesus as Savior and Lord we are embraced into the promise of this holy inheritance. The Church, as a corporate whole, shares a family relationship or kinship with each other. This corporate kinship is our birthright as born again believers and comes through the victory of the cross. When we choose Jesus as Savior and launch into our spiritual walk, God infuses us with His DNA. We have the opportunity to adopt the traits and characteristics available to our spiritual family as we mature.

As children of God, He adopts us and releases shared blessings. These are common traits shared by everyone in our spiritual family. This inheritance comes because we are joint heirs to the throne of God, living in the freedom and authority that comes through relationship with Christ. A corporate kinship is established through God's legacy creating a heritage that pulls us together through the bond of love.

Unpack it!

What does the term "corporate kinship" mean to you?

_____
_____
_____
_____

Have you ever considered that you have family connection with the whole body of Christ? Share your thoughts.

_____
_____
_____
_____
_____
_____
_____

Does recognizing your heavenly birthright change the way you see yourself? How do you live it out?

_____
_____
_____
_____
_____
_____
_____
_____
_____
_____
_____
_____

In what ways does this corporate kinship change the way you see others?

_____
_____
_____
_____
_____
_____
_____

Embrace it!

Lord, thank You for being a Father that loves His children so much that You adopt us and bind us together in love through Christ. You have accepted us and we are Your beloved. You gave us Your Holy Spirit to lead us on our journey without bondage or fear. You give us an inheritance that makes us heirs with Christ and solidifies our corporate kinship. Thank You, Lord, for being our perfect Father who abounds in perfect everlasting love!

Explore it!

Read Romans 8:14-17. You can pull out many important pieces of wisdom from these verses regarding shared inheritance. Break this section down line by line. Explore each line with the Lord and ask Him to reveal more about your birthright.

Read 1 Peter 2:9-10 and Ephesians 2:19-22. Compare and contrast the two sections of scripture. What are the similarities? What can you draw out of each section about your place in the Royal Priesthood of believers? Compare the images of being foreigners and strangers and being in darkness. What emotions rise up in you knowing you are adopted and embraced into a shared inheritance?

_____

Act on it! God placed treasures in this lesson. What treasure is He offering to you today? How do you think you might apply this treasure to your daily life?

Inheritance of Believers: Shared Identity 2

Stand on it! *"That the God of our Lord Jesus Christ, the Father of glory, may give to you the spirit of wisdom and revelation in the knowledge of Him, the eyes of your understanding being enlightened; that you may know what is the hope of His calling, what are the riches of the glory of His inheritance in the saints."* Ephesians 1:17-18

Think on it! Shared Identity Statements: In the last lesson we discussed how Jesus binds us together in a corporate kinship. Through this kinship, the body of Christ has common traits, promises and characteristics we share. Through the Bible, we can identify certain scriptures that pinpoint our shared identity. Each statement carries the inheritance specific to our place as believers in Christ and reminds us who we are in Christ. These scriptures can be written as identity statements for individuals and for groups within Christ. They remind us who we are individually, as well as what we share with our Christian family.

The identity statements below are a few of the many examples available in scripture. We can use Biblical truths in scripture to create these statements. The statements can be worded to apply to individuals and/or to the wider body of Christ.

"We are justified by grace." (Titus 3:7)
"We are more than conquerors." (Romans 8:37)
"We are seated with Christ in heavenly places." (Ephesians 1:20)
"We are heir to the blessings of Abraham." (Galatians 3:14)
"The Lord adopts and loves us." (Romans 5:25)
"I am holy and without blame before Christ." (Ephesians 1:4)
"I am blessed coming in and going out." (Deuteronomy 28:12)
"I am redeemed from the hand of the enemy." (Psalm 107:2)
"I have the spirit of wisdom, revelation and knowledge through Christ." (Ephesians 1:17)
"I am no longer a slave but am an heir as a son/daughter of Christ." (Galatians 4:7)

Unpack it!

Have you applied shared identity statements to your life? What was the result? If not, take one of the statements above to apply to your life right now!

_____
_____
_____
_____

What do you think a heavenly inheritance on earth looks like? What is included in this birthright?

_____
_____
_____
_____
_____
_____
_____
_____
_____
_____
_____
_____
_____
_____
_____

What does being a joint heir with Christ mean to you?

_____
_____
_____
_____
_____
_____
_____
_____
_____
_____
_____

Spend a few minutes speaking these statements out loud to the Lord. Did you speak them out with authority? If not, speak them out again with authority!

Embrace it!
Father, thank You for being a father that justifies me by grace and gives wisdom and revelation so I can know and understand more of You and who I am in You. Thank You, Lord, for giving me an identity of royalty that allows no lack but calls forth a life of abundance that is holy and without blame.
I praise You, merciful Lord!

Explore it!

Now it is your turn to practice finding and writing shared identity statements! Here is an example for you to see how identity statements can be pulled out from scripture.
Read Deuteronomy 28:12 *"The Lord will open to you His good treasure, the heavens, to give the rain to your land in its season, and to bless all the work of your hand. You shall lend to many nations, but you shall not borrow."*

This scripture covers areas of provision, prosperous/abundance, guidance and favor. Several identity statements can be written from this one verse. Examples would be as follows:

I am open to receive the treasures of the Lord.
The Lord provides my every need.
I am favored: receiving blessing for the work of my hands.
I am guided by the Lord every day.

Read Psalm 23. What verse or verses are the most meaningful to you? Take two of those verses and write at least two identity statements for yourself.

_____
_____
_____
_____
_____
_____
_____
_____
_____
_____
_____
_____
_____
_____
_____
_____
_____
_____
_____
_____
_____

"Reread 1 Peter 2:9-10 and Ephesians 2:19-22. These verses share about the corporate kinship we share with all believers. As you think about these verses, what shared identity statements can you draw out of these passages? Write them below and share them with a partner.

___

Act on it! God placed treasures in this lesson. What treasure is He offering to you today? How do you think you might apply this treasure to your daily life?

Inheritance of Believers: From Friend of God to Bride of Christ

Stand on it! *"Let us be glad and rejoice and give Him glory, for the marriage of the Lamb has come, and His wife has made herself ready."* Revelation 19:7

Think on it! In part 1 of this study, Journey to Identity: Foundation Building, we focused on knowing the personality and nature of God better. In our last few lessons, we discovered how to pinpoint our identities as the family of Christ. Now, we explore our personal identity, specific to who each of us is in Christ, and our personal journey and mission on earth.

As we move from friendship to a more intimate relationship with God, we move into a deeper connection with Him. Just like a dating relationship on earth, it is important to get to know each other as friends before the couple can step into the deeper intimacy of a marriage. A groom waits with anticipation as his bride walks down the aisle. As her hand is placed in his, he looks forward to the journey of discovery of who they are in each other. Their identity comes through being joined together as one, but they each maintain their individual gifts, personalities and talents. They have an identity as a couple, but are also uniquely designed for who God created them to be. Becoming the bride of Christ is similar, we find ourselves through our union with Him.

In a marriage we learn more about who we are because of the relationship and continual interaction with our spouse. In becoming the Bride of Christ, we also learn more about ourselves and areas of growth as His perfect love provides a safe place for growth, healing, and communication. The more confidence we have in who our Groom is, the more freedom we gain in exploring all God has for us. As we grow in relationship, Jesus points us toward our journey to fulfill the specific plans God created us to embrace.

Unpack it!

Have you ever thought about your relationship with God as preparation to be the Bride of Christ? If not, share some of your thoughts about this idea.

_____
_____
_____
_____
_____
_____

What is the value to your life in living as the Bride of Christ?

_____
_____
_____
_____
_____
_____
_____
_____
_____
_____
_____
_____

Where do you see your relationship with Jesus at this time? Servant, friend or bride?

_____
_____
_____
_____
_____
_____
_____
_____
_____
_____
_____

What steps can you take to become more intimately connected with Jesus?

_____
_____
_____
_____

Embrace it!

Lord, thank You that I am made perfect as I abide in You. As each day dawns I eagerly await for our time alone as I soak in Your loving Presence. You alone are the One I long for and I dream about our future together. The embrace of Your perfect love gives me comfort and peace. I no longer fear for I know that I am Your beloved.

Explore it!

Read Isaiah 54:4-5. Jesus is the bridegroom and we are the bride. Each of us is pictured as a beautiful bride who is loved and adored; accepted and beloved. The groom anxiously waits for the interaction that comes with the close relationship of a husband and wife. But just like in dating, the communication between both people is foundational to the strength of the relationship. Do you find yourself focusing on the regrets of your past; allowing the past regrets to become obstacles in your current relationship with Jesus? What if the energy you spend reflecting on the past was refocused on spending time with Him? Explore what changes or freedom might come in interaction with Jesus.

Read John 17:22-23. These verses highlight our permission to become unified in God. The process of our growth in being perfected, or coming into the fullness of our capacity as a believer in Christ, are offered as a promise for those who remain in Him. The growth only comes through continued connection to His presence. How does abiding, or staying in His presence bring change? What does "being perfected" mean to you? How does that process apply in your life, relationships or other areas of influence?

_____
_____
_____
_____
_____
_____
_____
_____
_____
_____
_____
_____
_____
_____
_____
_____
_____
_____
_____
_____
_____
_____
_____
_____
_____
_____

Act on it! God placed treasures in this lesson. What treasure is He offering to you today? How do you think you might apply this treasure to your daily life?

Personal Inheritance: Personal Identity

Stand on it! *"Your eyes saw my unformed body; all the days ordained for me were written in your book before one of them came to be."* Psalms 139:16

Think on it! God created each one of us with a unique design. No one else has the exact same combination of temperament, passions, skills and abilities you do! No one else on this earth is exactly like you. No one else has your fingerprint, DNA or exact voice. God looked at your unformed body and thought about His plan for you. As He began the formation process and considered what you were meant to accomplish, He thought about the people you would meet and the destiny calling He has written for your life. He created the specific traits you needed to fulfill your calling and bring His glory to all your areas of influence. Our deepest fulfillment comes in discovering the fullness of who we were created to be as He guides us toward His calling on our lives.

We cannot find our calling on our own, nor can we reach the fullness of our potential without growing in relationship with Him. He gives us the choice to journey toward the fullness of how He created us. Part of the way He made us requires that we walk beside Him and interact with Him in ever deepening ways. The maturing process and character growth allow us to grow in the authority He designed us to carry. He gives the tools and equips us to carry that authority with His grace and purpose, guiding us toward the fulfillment of the prophetic words He wrote in our "book of destiny."

You are specifically designed for the calling you have on your life. No matter how public or private that calling may seem to the world, heaven celebrates you as you step forward into that place of destiny and accomplish what He created you to do.

Unpack it!

Why do you think recognizing your unique design is important?

_____
_____
_____
_____
_____
_____
_____
_____
_____

What specific talents, skills and gifts can you pinpoint in you that you think are important to knowing who you are? In other words, what is your unique design?

_____
_____
_____
_____
_____
_____
_____
_____
_____
_____
_____
_____

How do you think knowing God allows you to understand yourself better?

_____
_____
_____
_____
_____
_____

What things have been revealed to you about yourself as your relationship with God has become more intimate?

_____
_____
_____
_____
_____
_____
_____

Embrace it!

Father, thank You for creating me completely different from any of Your other creations. I am a walking thumbprint made from Your DNA. Lord, open my heart so I will intuitively know what Your plan is for me as You guide me to fulfill my destiny. I awake each day with anticipation waiting for what You have for me! Your love and goodness never cease to overwhelm me and my heart is so full of love for You.

Explore it!

Read Psalm 139:13-18. Have you ever thought about the process of your personal creation? How does it make you feel to know how carefully you were made? What thoughts do you think God has about you? What dreams do you think He had when you were being created? Spend some time asking God these questions and write down your thoughts.

Read Ephesians 1:4-6 and 11-12. What does it mean to you to be called "holy and blameless?" Is this a free gift given by God or something you have to achieve? Do you see the purpose of your life glorifying Him? How has your relationship with God reoriented your life to His plan and purpose?

___

Act on it! God placed treasures in this lesson. What treasure is He offering to you today? How do you think you might apply this treasure to your daily life?

Personal Inheritance: Learning Who You Are / Inheritance

Stand on it! *"Now it happened on the third day that Esther put on her royal robes and stood in the inner court of the king's palace, across from the king's house, while the king sat on his royal throne in the royal house, facing the entrance of the house. So it was, when the king saw Queen Esther standing in the court, that she found favor in his sight, and the king held out to Esther the golden scepter that was in his hand. Then Esther went near and touched the top of the scepter. And the king said to her, "What do you wish, Queen Esther? What is your request? It shall be given to you--up to half the kingdom!"* Esther 5:1-3

Think on it! Esther put on her robes, stood in the inner court and found favor with the king. Just like Esther, you are clothed in the royal robes of righteousness and as a believer, stand in the inner court of the palace, or kingdom of God. The inner court represents a place of intimacy with your God and King. You have open access to Him as He has granted you favor to communicate with Him because of the reconciliation brought about through Jesus' death and resurrection. Just as Esther was offered up to half the kingdom, you are a co-heir to the kingdom and can access the inheritance that comes through that place of authority.

God is the Architect of your life. He knows your heart's desires. In fact, when He designed you, He placed those desires in your heart. As the Architect, He is excited to help you realize the fullness of who you were created to be. He delights in your learning process. He loves to talk about who you are and what He is calling you to do so that His glory/goodness can reach all the areas of influence you were created to touch.

As He talks with you, He speaks to you about your inheritance. Just like Gideon, Moses, and Abraham, He speaks to you as He sees you, not necessarily how you see yourself. As your relationship with God deepens, you will gain better insight about the inheritance of gifts, talents, authority and influence you carry as a child of the King.

Unpack it!

What are your thoughts of being an Esther? How does knowing you have Kingdom favor encourage you to claim your inheritance?

_____
_____
_____
_____

Can you identify any obstacles to understanding your identity and inheritance?
___

What do you see as your kingdom inheritance?
___

What do you think are the "heart's desires" God placed within you?
___

Embrace it!
Lord, You are the Architect of my life and I thank You for designing me in a way that my heart's desires are Your desires. I am not a pauper in Your kingdom, but Your child and co-heir to the throne! Let me hear Your voice calling me to rise up and walk as the person You designed me to be. I know that if You have called me You will equip me with what I need to carry that plan out. Thank You, Lord, for using me to carry Your glory into the world to help make a difference for Your kingdom.

Explore it!

Read Ephesians 2:10. Have you considered that you are a work of art? The way you are created by God included specific things He deposited in you as He made you. Your identity, or the way He sees you, points to your calling and the destiny He destined you to fulfill. How does knowing you were created for a specific purpose change the way you see yourself? How do you feel God has equipped you to walk in your calling?

Read Hebrews 11. Accepting Jesus as Savior, automatically insures an inheritance which is shared by all believers (see Shared Identity parts 1 and 2). But you also have a personal inheritance that includes *your* gifts, talents, skills and spiritual tools needed for *your* call. In this passage in Hebrews, the Bible goes through several major Biblical heroes of faith. For each one, identity statements are listed to describe their specific identity as they are known in heaven. Think about the specific identity you have. How do you think you are known in heaven? Write those thoughts down.

___

Act on it! God placed treasures in this lesson. What treasure is He offering to you today? How do you think you might apply this treasure to your daily life?

Personal Inheritance: Confidence In Identity

Stand on it! *"But rise and stand on your feet; for I have appeared to you for the purpose, to make you a minister and a witness both of the things which you have seen and of the things which I will yet reveal to you."* Acts 26:16

Think on it! When you step forward into ministry, whether it is a "formal" ministry or simply loving on those around you, you will meet resistance. That resistance may be internal or external. The only assurance you have in those situations is to remind yourself of who you are in Christ and that He has called you to a specific purpose.

The confidence you have in your identity in Christ and what He calls you to is vital for you to persevere through the challenges. The victories you have are important to recognize, celebrate and remember. Those victories build your confidence in your identity and reinforce the calling you have on your life. As you grow in identity confidence, you are able to stand on the promises of God and use them as weapons against any onslaught you face. Remembering who you are in Christ and knowing that you KNOW that you are designed for this purpose allows you to be a powerful voice of testimony and breakthrough.

As you spend time with God reaffirming your place in Him, the hunger you have for Him grows and you revel in His ability to open the doors of your heart and mind. The knowledge that He is vast draws you to Him. There is much more for Him to reveal. Knowing He directs and equips you as He leads you forward encourages a lifestyle of open dialogue with Him.

Unpack it!

How does knowing you are called by God to a certain area or gifting affect your confidence?

_____
_____
_____
_____
_____
_____
_____
_____

Why do you think confidence in your identity is vital to your walk in life?

Looking back through this study, how has your confidence grown in the nature of God and who you are in Him?

How does recognizing, celebrating and remembering the victories you have create confidence?

Embrace it!
Thank You heavenly Father for Your word that reminds me of who I am in You! Your word gives me confidence in my weakness knowing that You have designed and equipped me to carry out Your mission for my life. When the road ahead looks long and hard and I feel weary, Your word gives me strength.
I meditate on it day and night and find Your Holy Spirit reviving me so I can continue on my way! Knowing I can do all things through Christ and that You are with me always is all I need to persevere. I thank You, Holy Spirit, that You never leave me or forsake me, yet gently encourage me to move forward.

Explore it!

Read Philippians 1:6, 9-11. We are a work in progress. We are in a continual refining process that encourages the workmanship of Christ to come to fullness in us. What does Paul highlight as our responsibility in this process? How do you position yourself to embrace this process? What results out of this positioning? How do you think those results will look in your life and in your relationships with God and others?

_____

Read Ephesians 1:18-21. Knowing God promises to release the same power through you that He did through Christ's resurrection: Where do you see this power already active in your life and what breakthroughs are still available in your walk with God? How does learning to walk in more authority bring confidence in Him working through you?

___

Act on it! God placed treasures in this lesson. What treasure is He offering to you today? How do you think you might apply this treasure to your daily life?

Challenges in Identity: Dealing With Internal Negatives

Stand on it! *"For God has not given us a spirit of fear, but of power and of love and of a sound mind."* 2 Timothy 1:7

Think on it! One of the greatest battlegrounds we face is the one of our own insecurities. Those thoughts include lack, poverty, inability, unworthiness, etc. These self-limiting belief systems create personal limitations that promote fear and timidity in our lives. Often the source of a negative self-image comes from hurtful events or words spoken to us in our lives. Accepting those destructive words as truth create false identities and counteract your God given identity.

Those things that God opens to us are often discounted or even rejected because we have not embraced the truth of who He is and who we are in Him. What He opens to us and invites us into seems outside of our scope or ability. Rather than stepping into the process of refinement, knowing that refinement process requires us to stretch beyond our comfort zone, we retreat and stay where we "think" we control our surroundings.

Even though the enemy is the father of lies and continues to remind us of our insecurities, those who constantly focus on internal negative beliefs offer little threat to him and require minimal effort (on his part) to keep us there. Overcoming these detrimental beliefs require us to replace them (exchange) with God's truth each time they appear until we stop believing the lie and embrace the truth. For example replace the lie: "I am timid," with the truth: "I am bold," based on Philippians 1:20. Quoting scripture is one way to overcome.

Unpack it!

What self-limiting beliefs do you hear in your mind?

_____
_____
_____
_____
_____
_____
_____
_____
_____

How have those beliefs held you back from stepping into your true identity?

_____
_____
_____
_____
_____
_____
_____

What do you fear most about stepping out of your comfort zone? What keeps you from accepting the refining/stretching process in your life?

_____
_____
_____
_____
_____
_____
_____

Discuss some truths you can repeat to yourself each time you recognize a negative thought.

_____
_____
_____
_____
_____
_____

Embrace it!

Lord, I thank You that when the enemy tries to come and tell me his lies, You are there to remind me otherwise. You remind me that You created me fearless and wonderful. You created me with a purpose and have equipped me to achieve it with Your power that resides in me. I declare that I will no longer listen to the lies of the devil because I know that he is the father of lies and fear. Nothing good comes from him. Lord, I know that anything that You put before me can be done, for all things are possible with You! From this day forward, I renounce any fear, lies and disbelief about who You made me to be and I will walk in boldness, a co-heir to the King!

Explore it!

Read Acts 4:13 and John 21:15-19. Peter's negative thoughts and fear caused him to deny Jesus three times. He felt shame and had crawled back into his old life. However, Jesus redeemed and replaced those thoughts with Peter's commission, or calling, in John 15:15-19. Jesus meets with Peter in a loving way and reminded Peter of his true identity. Then, as Peter was empowered at Pentecost, he moved out with boldness and changed the world. Notice the pattern: Peter had negative beliefs, Jesus spent time with Peter and countered those beliefs with truth, and then Peter gained confidence in his identity and stepped into his destiny. What negative beliefs would you like to take to Jesus? What does He say to counter those lies with His truth (scripture, prayer, etc.)? How do these truths point to your identity? How does this process empower you to step forward into your calling?

_____
_____
_____
_____
_____
_____
_____
_____
_____
_____
_____
_____
_____
_____
_____
_____
_____
_____
_____
_____
_____
_____
_____
_____

Read Ephesians 3:16-20. God releases His glory to work in us and grants us permission to receive His unlimited riches. He empowers us to be filled with His fullness. He strengthens our identity and thought life as we walk closely with Him. How does that fullness allow you to overcome the internal battle? How does an expanded understanding of His unconditional love in your life establish a sound mind within you?

___

Act on it! God placed treasures in this lesson. What treasure is He offering to you today? How do you think you might apply this treasure to your daily life?

Challenges in Identity: Adversity and Identity

Stand on it! *"Be sober, be vigilant; because your adversary the devil walks about like a roaring lion, seeking whom he may devour."* 1 Peter 5:8

Think on it! Deepening your relationship with God and building confidence in your identity exist as important keys to overcoming any adversity that might come your way. Peter warns us that we have an enemy who wants to make us fail, but you have a choice on whether or not you allow him to rock your world.

Jesus encountered continuous challenges to His identity. From the moment He proclaimed Isaiah 61, which highlighted His identity and calling on earth, He faced adversity from all sides. No matter what He faced, He *knew* who He was (is) and whose He was (is). Even in the midst of betrayal and excruciating physical pain, He never wavered.

Knowing your identity creates an unshakeable confidence within you. Even in the midst of great personal challenge and seemingly insurmountable obstacles, the person who *knows* who they are and whose they are is harder to oppress. Hope of your calling remains and things that would try to distract you are more easily recognized and discounted. In fact, the very pressure intended to immobilize you will serve to refine your heart and strengthen your resolve for victory.

Unpack it!

Think of a time where you faced adversity and relied on your relationship with God to see you through that situation. How would having a stronger identity in Christ help you stand more effectively in that situation?

_____
_____
_____
_____
_____
_____
_____
_____
_____
_____

In our "Stand on it!" verse, the words "whom he *MAY* devour" opens the possibility that the devil has the ability to kill, but may not be able to complete his desire. How do you think a person with a strong sense of their identity and authority can resist the attempts of the enemy to harm them?

_____
_____
_____
_____
_____
_____
_____

How does knowing who you are and whose you are create a foundation that is difficult to shake?

_____
_____
_____
_____
_____
_____
_____

How does knowing your identity allow you to strengthen and refine in the midst of difficult circumstances?

_____
_____
_____
_____
_____
_____
_____

Embrace it!

Father, thank You for sending your son Jesus to die in place of me so that I can have authority over the enemy through the blood of Jesus. I do not have to walk in fear of the devil's evil schemes, but I can walk in confidence of who I am in Christ knowing that all things are possible with you, Lord! No matter what might come my way in life I know that Your Holy Spirit dwells in me and gives me the power to overcome trials and tribulations of this world. Lord, I pray that I will always be sober and vigilant never falling prey to the enemy but, instead, I am a mighty warrior for Christ!

Explore it!

Read Romans 8:28-29. Who does the scripture highlight to receive the "good?" How does knowing God's plan for your growth comfort you? How does that knowledge excite you? What do you think becoming more like Jesus means in regards to your personal identity? How does knowing God gave you a unique design give you confidence as you grow in Christ to fulfill the purpose for which He created you?

_____
_____
_____
_____
_____
_____
_____
_____
_____
_____
_____
_____
_____
_____
_____
_____
_____
_____
_____
_____
_____
_____
_____
_____
_____
_____
_____
_____
_____

Read James 1:5-6,12. God is an abundant giver. He gives freely to those who seek Him and the supply is not limited by our inadequacies. All of us will face challenges and difficult circumstance in life. We have a resource who offers a strategy to walk through and have victory in all those situations. How does doubt create instability? How much faith is required for God to give you wisdom? (Hint: read Matthew 17:20) According to the end of verse 5, will God condemn you or shame you for asking for His help? How does knowing this help you ask the Lord for help?

_____
_____
_____
_____
_____
_____
_____
_____
_____
_____
_____
_____
_____
_____
_____
_____
_____

Verse 12 highlights the importance of standing in faith during adversity. For every request God makes of us, He offers something specific for our success in that situation. What specific blessing have you seen God bring in difficult situations in your past? Think of an area of adversity you are currently facing. Make a list of the things you feel you need to have victory in that situation. Now take those requests before the Lord.

_____
_____
_____
_____
_____
_____
_____

Act on it! God placed treasures in this lesson. What treasure is He offering to you today? How do you think you might apply this treasure to your daily life?

Faith Walk: Faith Strengtheners / Altar Stone Memorials

Stand on it! *"Then he spoke to the children of Israel, saying: "When your children ask their fathers in time to come, saying, 'What are these stones?'"..."that all the people's of the earth may know the hand of the Lord, that it is mighty, that you may fear the Lord your God forever."* Joshua 4:21, 24

Think on it! The Lord established an amazing reminder of His majesty throughout the story of Exodus. At significant events on that journey, God instructed the Israelites to lay down altar, or memorial, stones to remind them and future generations of His sovereignty, provision, protection, majesty, presence, deliverance, etc. Later, the Israelites celebrated holy days (feasts) to remember those stones and remind themselves of God's promises. One pattern to note in the Exodus story is that as soon as another crisis came, the Israelites go back to grumbling and complaining that God is not with them or for them! Can you imagine what might have been lost without memorial stones and the creation of the feasts?

God established the reminder of the memorial stones to encourage Israel. He knew reciting the story of His intervention built faith in Him and His intentional heart toward Israel. He knew people got caught up in the moment of the latest crisis. He also knew that the reminder of memorial stones offered an opportunity to respond from a place of faith, instead of reacting emotionally.

We have memorial stones in our lives, too. They may not be physical rocks, but they exist as specific moments when we recognize God's presence moving in our lives. Unfortunately, many of us are not so different from the Israelites. Time moves on and the intensity of the moment fades as new life events require our focus. Our awe of God's intervention is pushed back or even forgotten. Our personal memorial stones build our faith and strengthen us in difficult times. Rather than reacting in fear, those personal memorial stones create a place for us to rise above the experience and remain steadfastly focused on Him.

Unpack it!

What events are your memorial stone moments?

_____
_____
_____
_____

Why do you think the move of God in our lives is so easy to forget?

_____
_____
_____
_____
_____
_____
_____

Why do you think identifying and remembering the memorial stones in your life are important to your relationship with God and your identity?

_____
_____
_____
_____
_____
_____
_____

Memorial stone moments are meant to be shared with others and our future generations. What makes these moments significant enough to share with others? How do you think future generations benefit from this information?

_____
_____
_____
_____
_____
_____
_____

Embrace it!

Lord, I pray that I am always aware of the meaningful moments when You come in like a flood to move in my life where changes are made on my behalf! Thank You, Lord, for being there even when I sometimes do not realize I need You or do not deserve Your abundant mercy. I cry out to You and You answer and strengthen my faith, O Lord! I always have these times to remind me of Your goodness and I am forever grateful as I rest in You.

Explore it!

Read Joshua 4. Through this passage, God lays out the reasons behind the memorial stones and the need for the generations to establish memorial testimonies and stories. As you read this passage, think about the important role testimony plays in our daily communication with others. In addition, think about the role your personal testimony plays in building your own faith in God and as confirmation of your identity in Christ. How has God confirmed your identity through these times of testimony? Have you ever considered how the power of God is released through the testimony you share? Write down what comes to mind and share that information with someone in your life.

Read I Corinthians 11:23-26 and Revelation 12:11a. Jesus established the new covenant and created the ultimate memorial stone for us as believers in Christ. By eating the bread and drinking the wine, we are, in effect, reminding ourselves of the love of Christ and the ultimate sacrifice of laying down one's life for another. What does this memorial stone provoke in you? What is the most significant memorial stone in your life outside of salvation?

_____
_____
_____
_____
_____
_____
_____
_____
_____
_____
_____
_____
_____
_____

In reading these passages what or who is overcome? Why does the blood of the Lamb overcome? Why does your testimony overcome? How does knowing that your testimony has power to help others give you confidence to share it? How does sharing your testimony build your faith in your present and future circumstances?

_____
_____
_____
_____
_____
_____
_____
_____
_____
_____
_____
_____
_____
_____

Act on it! God placed treasures in this lesson. What treasure is He offering to you today? How do you think you might apply this treasure to your daily life?

Faith Walk: Destiny Calling

Stand on it! *"It is the Spirit who gives life; the flesh profits nothing. The words that I speak to you are spirit, and they are life."* John 6:63

Think on it! As you walked through this journey to identity, you have been given all God created you to be to strengthen and expand your spiritual foundation. This journey is not over. In fact, it has just begun. The confidence you gain in your identity of how to flourish during adversity, building memorials of faith and exchanging internal negatives for His truth build your perception of who you are in Christ. Deciding to pour into time with God and two-way conversations with Him take you to new places of depth and surety of your place in His kingdom.

What's the next step? Combining who you are in Christ with your life's testimony point to your destiny calling. What is a destiny calling? It is the specific area of influence for which the Lord designed you. This is found by combining your understanding of who you are with areas of your life over which you have gained victory. These two things supported by your expanding relationship with God catapult you into a place where you recognize the fullness of who you are. You reach a place where you know that you know you are walking on the path God placed before you. And you have the peace that comes in recognizing you were made for this!

Destiny calling sounds like a big thing to bite off, but it is really a series of small steps. As you actively remain in Him and learn to receive all He has for you while in His presence, you gain perspective of how He views things around you. You learn to listen to His leading and direction and are able to move forward into a greater sense of His love for you and for others. The ministry, or destiny calling, you have in your life is merely an overflow of your relationship with Him. He fills you and, because He delights in abundance for you, He continues to pour into your heart to the point you cannot contain it any longer. It overflows to others. Your influence to others becomes a flash flood of encounter with Him.

Unpack it!

List/Share your areas of victory.

_____
_____
_____
_____

Describe your identity as you currently understand it.

_____
_____
_____
_____
_____
_____
_____
_____
_____
_____
_____

What do you feel is your destiny calling?

_____
_____
_____
_____
_____
_____
_____
_____
_____
_____
_____

Where can you begin to actively influence others around you?

_____
_____
_____
_____
_____
_____
_____

Embrace it!
Father, thank You for an anointing that empowers me to walk in my destiny calling. You are the Great I Am who never leaves me nor forsakes me. I sit at your feet Lord and bask in Your glory as I grow in the knowledge of who I am through You. I arise and step out in faith towards Your still small voice that is forever calling me to be all that I am in You.

Explore it!

Read I John 2:24-27 and John 6:45. These verses describe the role of Father, Son and Holy Spirit. In I John 2:27, the Holy Spirit is designated as your teacher. His role is to keep you from deception and to empower you. A great picture is to see yourself sitting at the feet of Jesus, knowing the words you hear are brought to you through the presence of Holy Spirit in your life. He brings wisdom to understand the mysteries of the things Jesus and the Father reveal to you. What do you think it means to remain, stay or abide, in Christ? In these verses, the work is placed on the Lord. What is your role in that process of abiding? According to these verses, do you have to figure it out or does the Lord open it up to you? Do you feel any additional freedom in knowing that the Lord taught the prophets this way? What liberty comes to your life knowing your role is to receive and God has put the responsibility on Himself to teach you His truth? Write down your thoughts.

Read 1 Peter 1:3-10. Our faith in Him opens up a new world of inheritance for us. As we continue to grow in relationship with Him, our faith has no option but to increase. These heavenly blessings are reserved for you to use on earth, not to receive once you get to heaven. What good are they then? The inheritance is part of what Jesus indicates as God's kingdom coming on earth as in heaven in the Lord's prayer. Our birthright provides spiritual tools and revelation that transform our hearts and then that transformation is witnessed by others; providing opportunity to share testimony of God's love and presence in our lives. However, the transformation process is a gradual shift. The journey continues throughout your whole life on earth. What spiritual tools does God release to you as your birthright? What transformation have you experienced through this study? How does your inheritance help you step into your destiny calling?

_____
_____
_____
_____
_____
_____
_____
_____
_____
_____
_____
_____
_____
_____
_____
_____
_____
_____
_____
_____
_____
_____
_____
_____
_____
_____
_____

Act on it! God placed treasures in this lesson. What treasure is He offering to you today? How do you think you might apply this treasure to your daily life?

About the Authors

Christine Casten, founder of Radiant Ministries International, is an ordained minister who speaks locally, nationally and internationally. A dynamic and interactive presenter, her passion is to see each person in the body of Christ rise to walk in the purpose of his/her calling. Her focus incorporates tools to discover and embrace our Christian identities along with "grace for the process" of spiritual growth. Christine's passions include helping others pinpoint the purpose of his/her calling and direction of God's leading. She activates the body through speaking, mentor-coaching, writing, and ministering. For more connect to www.radiantministries.org

Shelley White is passionate about having an intimate relationship with the Lord and knowing Biblical truths that bring freedom from negative mindsets. Shelley teaches Biblical insights that help set the captives free and find their true identity in Christ. Her main areas of focus are teaching, training, mentoring and developing tools for pulling God's truth out of His word. She has a heart for global missions and loving on God's children around the world. After twenty five years as a flight attendant she retired and practices real estate in the Dallas Metroplex and loves to teach others about the kingdom of God. She is the founder of Kingdom Minds Ministry. She and her husband Robert live in McKinney, Texas and all together they have six children, three love in laws, and a fifth grandbaby on the way! www.kingdomminds.com

The Story Behind All God Created You to Be

Christine and Shelley have been friends for several years. They often get together to catch up, bounce ideas off each other and discuss life and ministry. This particular day found them sharing over a couple of hot mugs.

Shelley was looking for a study. She hoped to find one on Christian identity and asked Christine if she had stumbled across any. Both actively mentor and are always on the look out for new material. They were challenged to find studies that encouraged the maturing process beyond foundational teaching. Although most Bible studies offer fabulous tools to establish Christian beliefs, many of the people they mentor/coach already have a great foundation in place! Both Christine and Shelley look for studies that help build on those strong foundations, especially in the area of Christian identity.

Why is identity such an important topic for both of them?

Christine spent years "trying" to be a good Christian. But, at the end of the day, she was just tired and was missing an important key for maturing in her faith. She entered into a two-year sabbatical and focused on biblical study and prayer to seek the Lord for better understanding. During this time, the Lord revealed the missing key…identity. God brought people into her life who, like Christine, were believers and were grounded in the Bible, but were looking to mature as Christians. Identifying and embracing their unique identities proved to be the key they were missing, too. Helping people and groups discover their unique identities in Christ became one of Christine's passions. Through one on one mentoring and interaction with others through conferences and training seminars, Christine realized many do not know how to discover the unique way God created them. She helps people look beyond gifting and call to open a deeper understanding of God's heart and to build confidence in who they were created to be.

Shelley faced challenges finding curriculum about Identity in Christ. Through mentoring others and in her own journey, she studied the Bible, read many books and pored through Bible studies to grow and learn. She often found herself "hungry" for more and spent countless hours learning the Word and with the Lord. Through her life journey, she had learned that what the world had to offer was empty. The Lord showed her that seeing herself through His eyes and through His word reveals her value and worth. She knows that she is never alone and is fully embraced by the love of God as she continues to walk along this path of life. Shelley's story is a part of her God given identity and she shares it freely as she teaches and mentors others in their discovery of their own identity in Christ.

So, what do to? Where could they find a study? "Why don't we write one?" Christine and Shelley joked. But, over the next few days, God confirmed this was exactly what He wanted them to do! The journey began. They set aside the time and met weekly to work on writing the study. As always, God amazed them in how much He blessed that time. Now, you get the opportunity to experience this part of the journey with them and learn more about All God Created You to Be!

Your Turn!

We would love to hear more about YOUR experience with
All God Created You to Be: A Journey to Identity!

- Share the story of how God touched your heart through this study.

- Let us know how the questions and application exercises in this study helped your Christian growth.

- Want to know more about Christine Casten and/or Shelley White? This site also contains links to each of their ministries. Connect to teachings, blogs and more.

Go to the website at www.allgodcreatedbook.com.